ALPHA SOUP LAND

As Mapped by
Fred Aura the
Explorer

Biological Sex Citadel

QUEENDOM

Whatever Waters

Agender Pass

TRANS LANDS

The Fairy Jar

Peaks of Personal Introspection

River of Representation

The Phallic Palace

Drag Docks

Cross dressing Cove

Non-Binary Bay

Femme fields

ch Beach

GULF of ALTERNATIVE GENDER

Genderqueer Riptides

EXPRESSION

ROMANCE

GENDER

SEXUALITY

'M'inority Monsters

AKA Fred Aura's Adventures in ALPHABET SOUP LAND

Minority Monsters

Published by Khaos as part of Discord Comics

Printed in the UK   First printing March 2017   ISBN 978-0-9570403-8-0

Welcome to Alphabet Soup Land
Listen, learn, try to understand
These stories of diversity
Behind these myths you will see
Minority Monsters like you and me,
Like you and me...?

Editor's Foreword
by Tab Kimpton

Alphabet Soup Land is a previously lost island in the middle of the Rising Seas of Representation. People always knew it existed but were scared to speak its name, and it's only now after years of civil rights movements and legal battles that we're starting to encounter citizens of this land living openly among us. Historically they were always there, but the fear of their unique magic drove them to hide, only expressing themselves in safe company without fear of reprisal.

In the human realm we frequently refer to the misunderstood monsters of Alphabet Soup Land as Lesbian, Gay, Bisexual and Transgender. However recent research has shown that the acronym LGBT barely scratches the surface of the variety, diversity and queerness of the creatures who inhabit the island.

The following pages contain the research notes of Fred Aura the Explorer who ventured into Alphabet Soup Land, never to return. That makes it sound very morbid- he didn't disappear without a trace or any such nonsense; he's currently alive and well, exploring deeper into the hidden depths that gender, sexuality and romance hold. We exchange postcards quite often.

These notes are but a brief summary of all the flamboyant, fabulous and fantastical beasts he encountered during his first research trip. You can read it like an adventure, discovering along with Fred during his journey, or use the index at the back to look up particular topics. Even if you're a minority monster yourself or are already savvy with sexuality there's always something new to learn. I didn't realise how little I knew myself until I edited it all together... but that's the nature of this beast. These monsters are always evolving and I'll be delighted to see what new creatures are discovered in my lifetime.

So grab your open mind and set sail through the Ocean of Alternative Gender, dock your boat in the Drag Docks, splash through the River of Representation, pass through the Peaks of Personal Introspection, ogle at the Orchard of Temptation and hike the Homo Hills to the Flamboyant Forest where we will encounter our first beast:

Sir Fabulous the Third
The Bisexual Unicorn

Happy exploring!
-Tab

SIR FABULOUS
THE THIRD
THE
BISEXUAL
UNICORN

BISEXUAL
UNICORNS

Bisexuals are attracted to their own gender AND to genders not their own

Bisexual started as a medical term between HETEROSEXUAL (opposite attraction) and HOMOSEXUAL (same attraction)

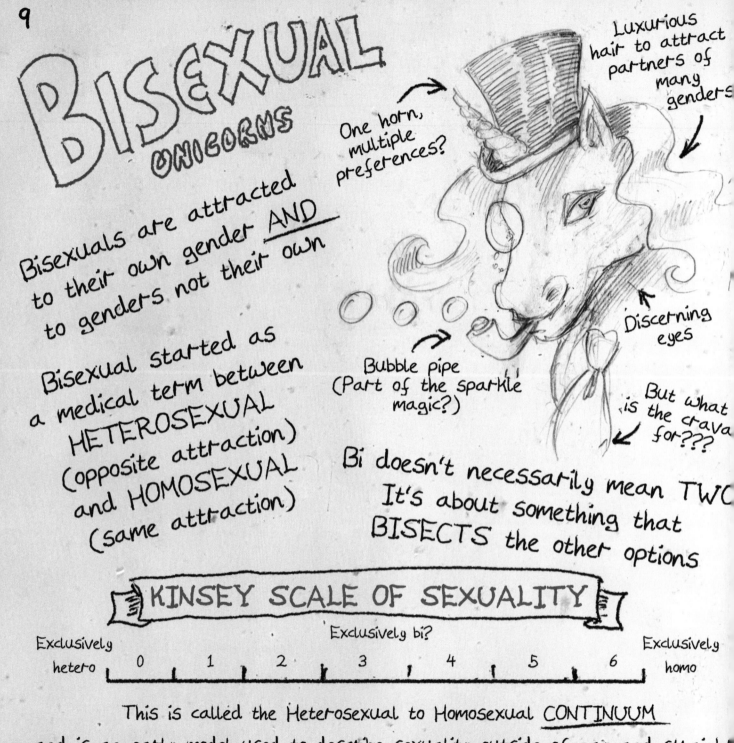

One horn, multiple preferences?

Luxurious hair to attract partners of many genders

Discerning eyes

Bubble pipe (Part of the sparkle magic?)

But what is the cravat for???

Bi doesn't necessarily mean TWO
It's about something that BISECTS the other options

KINSEY SCALE OF SEXUALITY

Exclusively hetero

Exclusively bi?

0   1   2   3   4   5   6

Exclusively homo

This is called the Heterosexual to Homosexual CONTINUUM
and is an early model used to describe sexuality outside of gay and straight

COMMON MYTHS

* Bisexuals are just confused

* Bisexuals have to like every gender equally in order to get their Bisexual Gold Card

* The sparkles exuded by Bisexuals when they brush their luxurious hair is the reason why the stars shine at night

* If you figure out how to break the Hetero-to-Homo Sexual Continuum you will have the ability to travel through time and space

* Bisexuals will never commit to one partner because they always need to date someone of each gender

Not to be confused with POLYAMORY ...

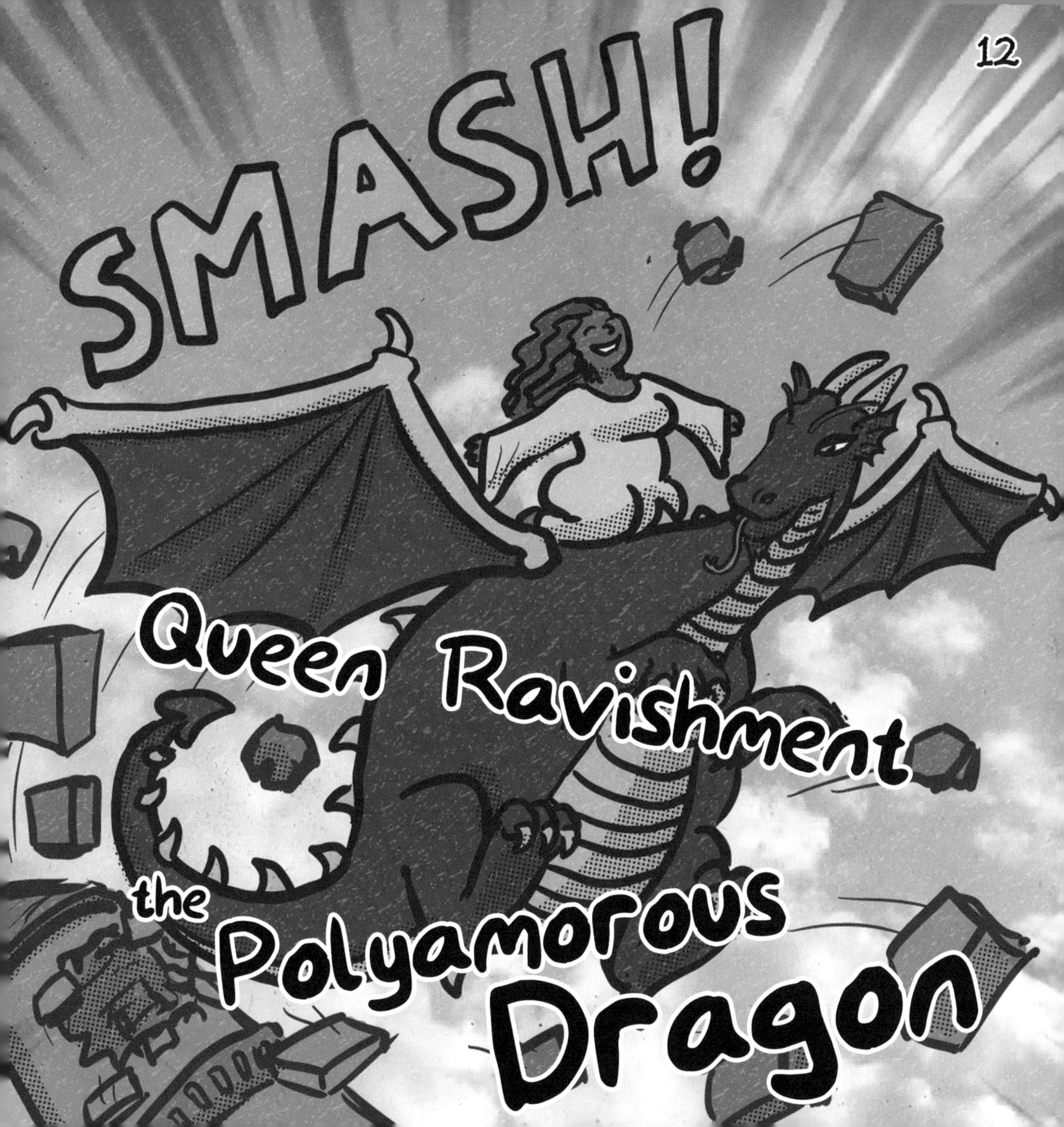
SMASH!
Queen Ravishment
the Polyamorous Dragon

POLYAMORY & DRAGONS
(MANY LOVES)

The desire (and practice) of multiple relationships with the consent of all people (and monsters) involved. NOT CHEATING.

AKA Consensual Non-monogamy

Comes in many forms:

Sometimes all people are together

Sometimes one person has multiple partners

Sometimes things get more complicated

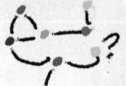

Like the Dryad Triad

Some have a Don't ask, Don't tell policy wit partners, some need to know more details.

The Poly Symbol of Infinity
Each relationship is unique to the monsters in it, so there are infinite ways to be poly.

COMMON MYTHS:

* Poly people are just greedy and hoard their partners like gold

* Polyamorists have multiple invisible hands so they can hold hands with all their partners at once

* It is forbidden for poly monsters to ever get jealous

BEWARE OF JEALOUSY DRAGONS

While there is no limit to the amount of love a person can give there is a limit to the amount of time they have. (unless you're an immortal dragon I guess)

Thick scales for ignoring society expectations

Long tongue for communicating boundaries

But some creatures ARE interested in monogamy...

MULTIPLE HEARTS
MULTIPLE LOVES

HOMOSEXUAL

(OR GAY GRIFFINS)

Someone attracted to people the same gender as themselves. But more than friends- like, in a GAY way.

A mix of sexual, romantic and social behaviour...

Gay has come to mean <u>much</u> more than just who you like to have sex with.

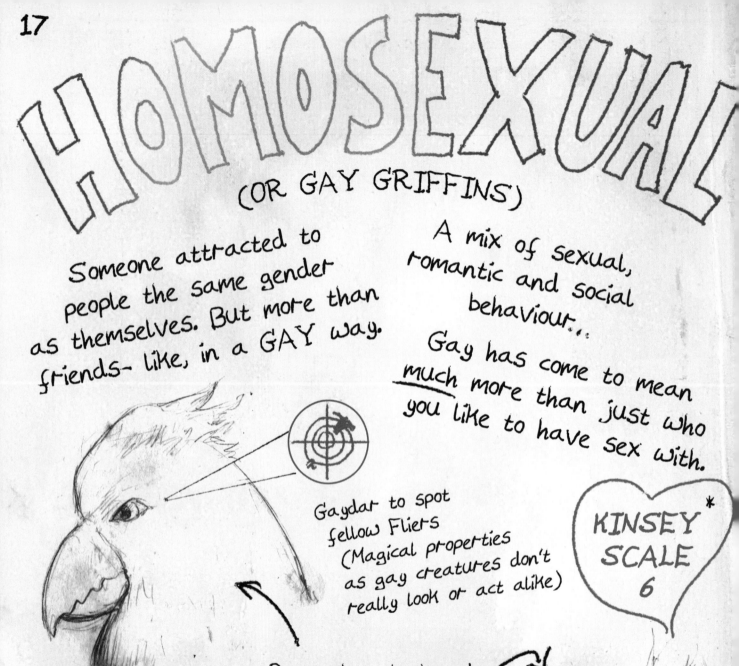

Gaydar to spot fellow Fliers (Magical properties as gay creatures don't really look or act alike)

KINSEY SCALE 6 *

Fluffy down for fluffy feelings of same sex romance

Razor sharp beak and claws to protect from DISCRIMINATION

HETEROFLEXIBLE

(NOT-QUITE-STRAIGHT HIPPOGRIFFS)

Generally heterosexual but with the occasional exception

Sometimes you just find a fellow bird of a feather!

On a similar spectrum as the Homoflexible Hippocampus

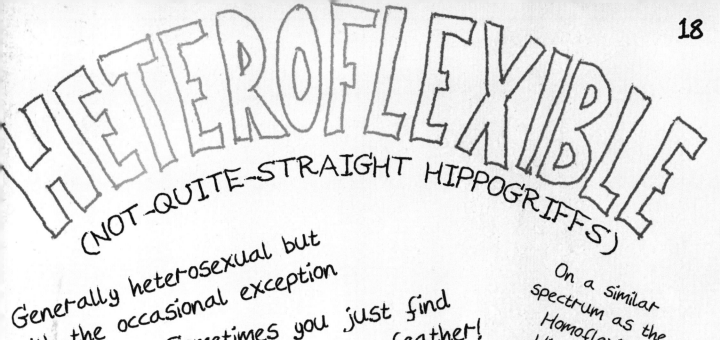

Sleek feather lines to show fluid nature of sexual attraction

KINSEY SCALE 2 *

Beak, hooves AND claws

Beasts on this spectrum often face discrimination from both the Heterosexual and Homosexual community.

* For more info on the Kinsey scale see Bisexual Unicorns on page 9

Sometimes even bad assumptions from their own partners...

Translation: Gary, I love you, will you be with me forever?

I don't know Hank- you're hetero-flexible and I'm not your usual type.

What if you're never satisfied with me?

Gary, just because I normally like hippochicks doesn't mean I can't be monogamous with you.

Reverend Tumbles the Pansexual Satyress

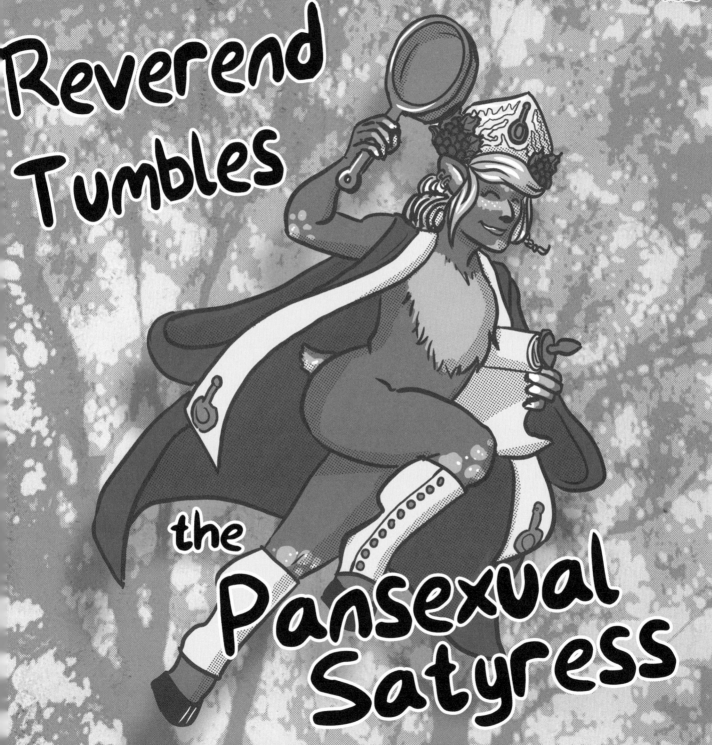

PANSEXUAL
(SATYRS, SATYRESSESS AND FAUNS)

Someone who is attracted to people regardless of their gender

From the Disciples of the Greek God Pan- the patron of wine, feasting and multi-gendered orgies

Not about frying pans

(Strangely appropriate symbol though)

THE MIGHTY MITRE OF PANDOM

useful snack?

Part of the polysexual principalities along with bisexual

A freckle for every gender they'r attracted to

COMMON MYTHS

* Pan monsters just want everyone to be pansexual like them

* Pansexuals are SO attractive they have to beat people off with frying pans (well, this might be true)

* Pan creatures are just attention-seeking special snowflakes

* Pansexuals are just sluts

* Pan people get hard frying eggs

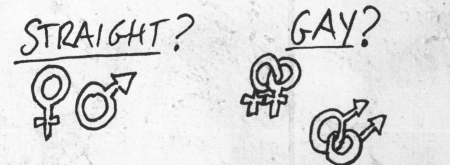

STRAIGHT?   GAY?   PAN

But of course there are some creatures
who don't like anyone THAT way . . .

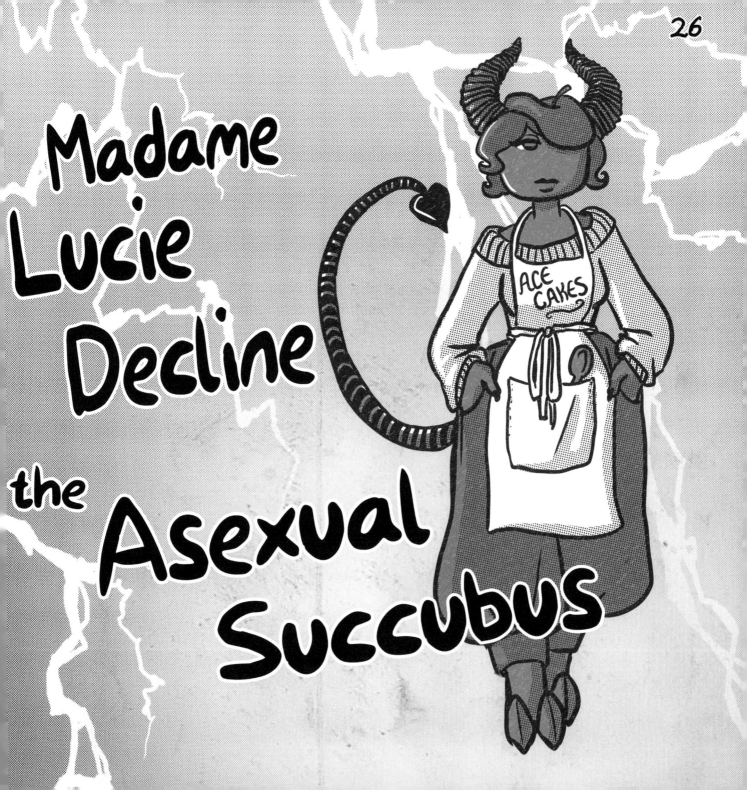

ASEXUAL
(SUCCUBI)

"A" for an absence of sexual interest...

...not because they reproduce by splitting themselves (like starfish!)

Might have horns, doesn't mean they're horny. →

Hidden ears as they're tired of listening to opinions about their private sex lives. ↗

PREFERS CAKE

TO SEX?

To be fair, it is excellent cake...

Different to chastity and abstinence - it's about a lack of sexual feelings, not about choosing not to.

It's common sense! If some people are really into sex, some people must be really NOT into it.

COMMON MYTHS

* Asexuals just need to find the RIGHT monster to fix them. (ew)

* Asexual creatures are cold hearted creatures and just want the human race to die out

* Ace beasts are total cheaters at poker due to their summoning abilities for certain cards...

A SUIT FOR ALL ACES?

Some asexuals do have sex, often because it pleases their partner. This doesn't change who they are.

Some asexuals hate sex completely and consider themselves "Sex averse". (Like how some people can't stand mint chocolate chip cupcakes.)

Some asexuals are interested in romance, others are not. There's even a special word to describe that Kind of creature...

ACE OF HEARTS

ACE OF SPADES

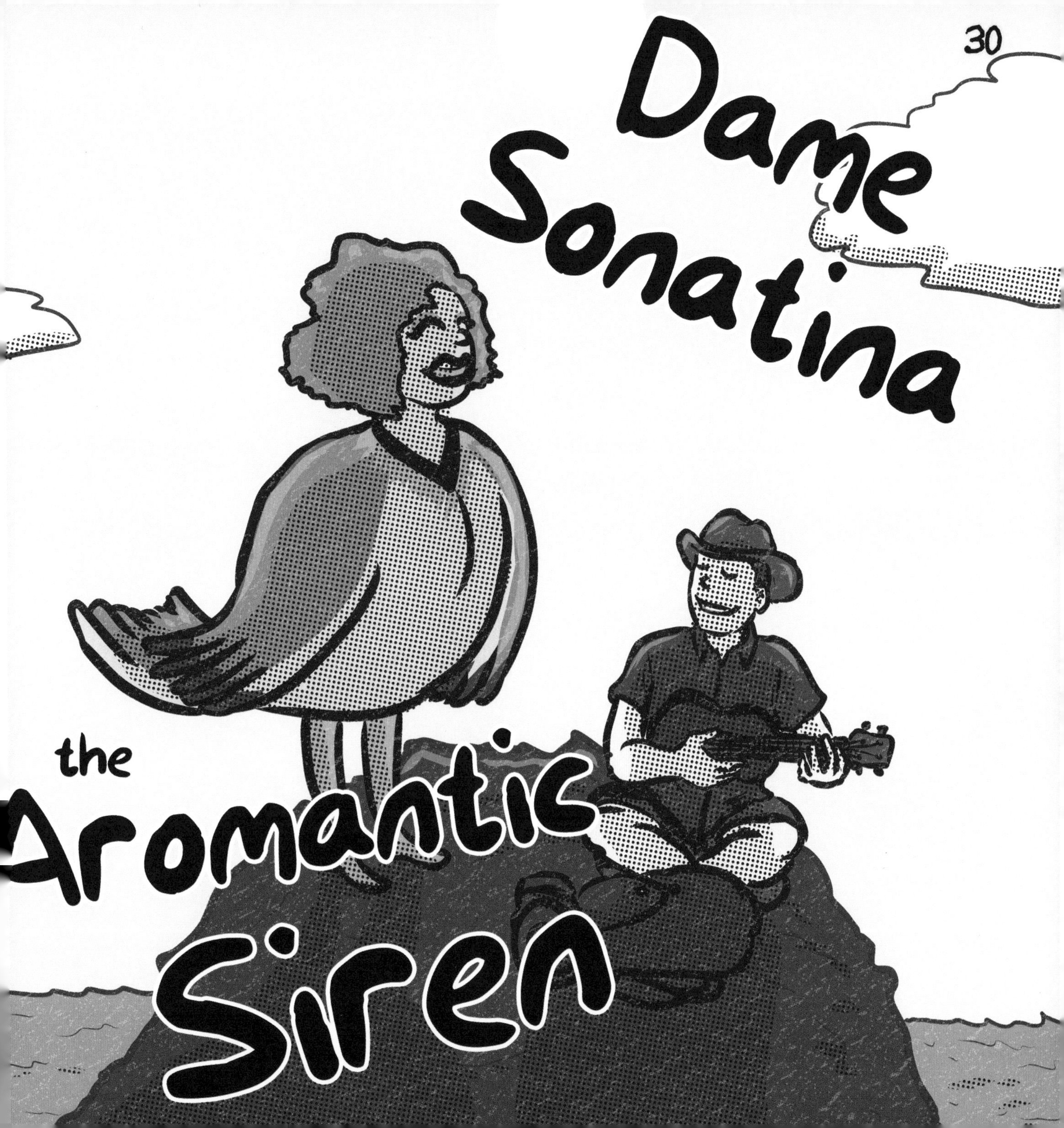
Dame Sonatina
the Aromantic Siren

AROMANTIC
SIRENS

Someone who isn't romantically attracted to others.

These creatures are satisfied with friendships and other non-romantic connections and live fufilling lives without the search for twoooo love

Strong legs because she's a strong, independent bird who don't need no greek hero.

Attractive plumage- not single due to a lack of interested partners!

Operatically trained lungs used to shouting "I'm not into you THAT way!"

A COMMON MYTH
Single people are all miserable

SEXUAL VS ROMANTIC ATTRACTION

A venn diagram of different types of attaction

ROMANTIC

Flowers!

Dancing in the moonlight

movies

Special gifts

PLATONIC

BFF bradlettes

Gals being pals

Getting married?

Hugging

fuck buddies!

Naked hugging?

XXX naked times

Squeezing bums?

SEXUAL

This varies a lot from person to person.

What's the difference between platonice, sexual and romantic to you?

The difference between
"Do I like this person,"
"Do I like-like this person" and
"Do I want to climb them like a tree?"

Fukkit

the Demisexual Demigod

DEMISEXUAL
DEMIGODS

GREY-A
GARGOYLES

Someone who does not feel sexual attraction until they form a strong connection with someone

Creatures who sit in the grey area between asexual and sexual

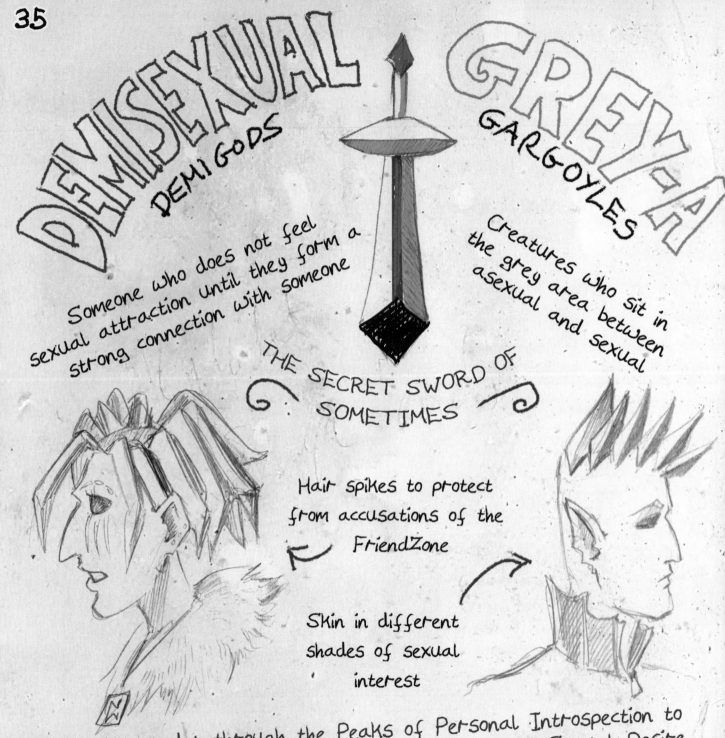

THE SECRET SWORD OF SOMETIMES

Hair spikes to protect from accusations of the FriendZone

Skin in different shades of sexual interest

Now let's wander through the Peaks of Personal Introspection to the deadly sands of the Desert of Sexual Desire . .

Baroness Camp Von Glamour the Lesbian Harpy

Powerful wing muscles

LESBIAN
HARPIES

A woman (or other female creature) who is only attracted to other women.

Lesbian as a word comes from the Island of Lesbos where the lady-loving-lady Poet Sappho lived in 600BC.

FEMME

A queer person with a feminine gender identity and expression. First used within Lesbian communities as a contrast to Butch . . .

Sharp teeth to fend off straight men who can't take the hint

Seal of Sappho

GAY VALKYRIES

Originally means "carefree" "joyful" or "bright and showy"

Gay is someone who is romantically and sexually attracted to their own gender

Boob shield maidens?

Gay women are often referred to as lesbians, but not everyone identifies with that.

BUTCH

A woman who is masculine in appearance but still identifies as female

HEL'S ANGELS

The gay community has played a large role in leather subculture

This is sometimes mixed up with Trans men . . .

King Monarch

the Trans Ex-Princess

TRANSGENDER
KINGS, QUEENS AND OTHER ROYALTY.

Transgender is an umbrella term for anyone who has a gender identity different from their assigned sex.

This includes people who transition from male to female (or vice versa) as well as people who don't identify as either.
(but more on that later)

When they were born the doctor shouted "It's a girl!" but as they got older they started to realise it wasn't true.

King Monarch is open about growing up a princess, but many trans people are NOT and that should be respected.

Sometimes this is for safety reasons- trans people often get fired, harassed or are the subjects of violenc

Antennae for deep personal introspection

Long hair a symbol of age and wisdom

Some people use -anssexual to describe those who medically transition from one gender o the other, but this word is falling out of favour.

(Possibly because it makes it sound like a sex thing when it's actually about gender)

In the human realm about 1/1000 people identify as transgender.

Unfortunately non-magic folk can't just drink a potion to magically change how they look.

Instead, people use a combination of hormones, clothes and surgery to make their bodies match their minds.

– I'm ME!

TRANSGENDER ROYAL SEAL

A mixture of the Venus and Mars symbols

And some people are born with bodies not typically described as male or female to begin with . . .

Izzy

the Intersex Incubus

INTERSEX

PEOPLE, CREATURES AND MEDICAL DEMONS

Someone who is born with a body that does not fit typical definitions of male or female.

LET'S TALK ABOUT SEX, BABY

Horns of Mercury

Gender of choice

Body of none of your business

Tail of Venus

When we talk about biological sex what we're REALLY talking about is...

* External genitalia (Visible bits)

* Levels of Testosterone, Estrogens, Progesterone and other sex hormones

* Whether they have ovaries or testicles

* Internal reproductive organs (like the uterus)

* Chromosomes (XX, XY, XXY and several other variations)

I've heard the word 'Hermaphrodite' before - how does that fit into this?

We get the word from Hermaphroditus, the son of the gods Hermes and Aphrodite, who was portrayed in ancient art as having a female figure and male genitals. We now know that sex is much more beyond the bits on the outside, so Intersex was coined in the 1920s.

Are intersex people trans/gay?

Some of them are, some aren't, just like everyone else. Intersex people are often included in LGBT but face different problems such as invasive doctors and non-consensual surgery on their genitals as children . . . just because adults want to be able to put either M or F on a birth certificate.

But surely doctors know best?

Yes . . . but what if they get it **wrong?**

Unless it's medically necessary, it's much better to wait until the person is older and can make the choice about their own body.

Wait . . . I've never had my chromosones tested! Does that mean I could be intersex and never know?

Yep! A lot of people never even find out unless something comes up medically in later life.

Now you're ready to dive into the Ocean of Alternative Gender...

Captain Sashay the Genderqueer Merperson

GENDERQUEER
MERPEOPLE

Someone who identifies with neither,
both or a combination of male and female

We know from learning
about Intersex people that bodies
come in many different
combinations

So it makes sense that some
people have minds which don't fit in
either category too.

Green skin as it's a
colour not associated
with any abitrary
gender (like blue
and pink)

Gold! Always
believe in your
souuulll

Unfortunately outside of Alphabet Soup Land, society has
a hard time understanding and swimming through the
Gulf of Alternative Gender . . . .

It helps if you stop thinking of male and female as opposites

But more like a set of traits people can identify with and express themselves as.

MALE ——————— FEMALE

And it's more than just a spectrum

There are entire seas of expression, identity and social conventions to explore

NEUTRAL

The water's fine!

MALE

FEMALE

PART OF THE TRANSGENDER UMBRELLA

Genderqueer itself is an umbrella term for many other types of monsters

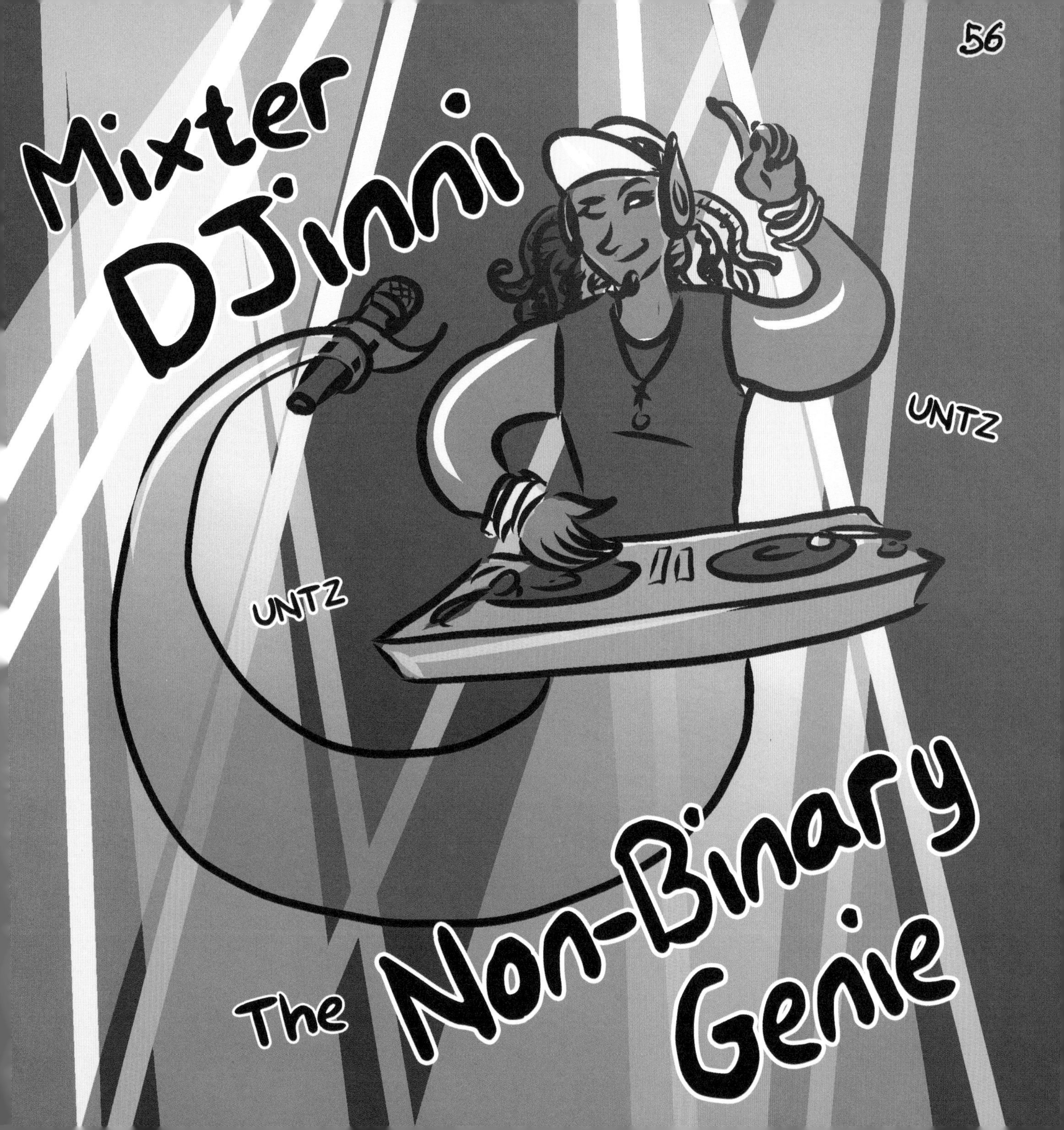
Mixter
DJinni
UNTZ
UNTZ
The Non-Binary Genie

NON BINARY

GENIES, DJINNIS AND OTHER JINN

Gender identity which does not fit into the Male and Female Binary

Symbol a combination of Male, Female and 'X' for None, Neither and Not Applicable

The Gender Binary is the idea that there are only two options: Man or Woman.

0 1 0

Binary code is how computers work. It's 0's and 1's or On and Off.

10   0 1

11

Gender Roles are the idea th our genitals decide how w behave, the things we like and what we should do.

But humans (and other creatures) are made up of so **much** more than that.

COMMON MYTHS

* If you free a Non Binary monster from the Gender Matrix they'll become a kung fu master and overthrow their robotic overlords

* Non Binary Creatures only collect music on vinyl

Rub the lamp of gender enlightenment!

NON BINARY NEUTRAL TITLES

Mixter

Mx

Dr

Captain

Mastress

Professor

Reverend

President

Your Honour

The Honourable

Their Royal Highness

HOW TO HONOUR HONOURIFICS

Our language reinforces the idea that there are only two options (and no in between) by our very titles.

Mr

Miss
Mrs   Ms

Mx or Mixter is gaining awareness as an option though, and is legally recognised in several countries in the human world.

(Unfortunately, many of the other titles on the list require some serious qualifications to earn.)

Maybe a Gender Professor can shed some more light on this . . .

AGENDER
SPHINXES, SPHINGES AND OTHER RIDDLES

Who nose what gender they are?

Well, the answer is, they don't really have one.

Agender means someone who doesn't identify with a gender at all.

Genderless, genderfree, non-gendered, lacking gender, neutrois, neutral. . .

Agender is a word for people who don't feel described by definitions of gender

Very sharp teeth (hopefully due to a hunger for knowledge, not human flesh)

Professor Puce enjoys educating people, but don't expect the same of all other creatures!

* Agender creatures can't wear any colour besides beige in case it's deemed too masculine or feminine by the gender police

* Agendered monsters think gender sucks and won't let any genderedpeople into their non-boys-girls-or-other clubhouse

* If an agendered, asexual and aromantic person beats you up it's called a Triple A Battery

* Agendered people have to look like a genderless void to be worthy of their official title

BUT HOW CAN I BE POLITE IF I CAN'T TELL AN AGENDERED PERSON BY JUST LOOKING AT THEM?

Have you tried... Asking?

And if you get it wrong, just apologise and try to get it right next time

Mx Alex the Gender fluid Phoenix

GENDERFLUID

PHOENIX(ES)

Someone who doesn't have a fixed gender identity

This can be someone who moves distinctly from one gender to another

(AKA bigender, trigender and pangender)

or generally just fluctuates between male, female, both and neither.

Careful- the hair feathers burn if you attempt to touch without asking!

A COMMON MYTH

* If people don't stay the same gender for their entire life society itself will collapse and bring about Gendertropy

Likes coffee so hot it's on fire

PROPER PRONOUNS

Pronouns are the words we use to talk about others

HE/HIM/HIS

Traditionally Male

THEY/THEM/THEIRS

Plural and Neutral
(Also good if you're not sure
and don't want to offend!)

SHE/HER/HERS

Traditionally female

THE BEST WAY TO SHOW PROPER RESPECT TO ALL KINDS OF CREATURES IS TO USE THE RIGHT GENDER WORDS FOR THEM

But the English Language is a bit rubbish with neutral pronouns.

While "They" is most common it can get confusing
if someone thinks you're talking about more
than one person

Here's a list of some of the less common neutral
pronouns people use to try to fix this problem.

Ey/em/eirs
E/Em/Eirs
Xe/xem/xyrs
Sie/hir/hirs
Ve/ver/vis
Ze/zir/zirs
Ne/nem/nirs
Ze/zer/zers

English has changed so much that it will
be interesting to see how it adapts as we
learn more about alphabet soup land.

After all, gender is somewhat decided
by the society we live in . . .

GENDER AND

What did the warrior/worrier mean by society?

Well, what counts as "masculine" or "feminine" depends on the time, culture and specific location of the people involved . . .

Boys wear "skirts" all over the world

KILT   KURTA   SARONG

Makeup has been used by women, gods and men all through the ages

Some of the first pioneers of computer programming were women

ADA LOVELACE   GRACE HOPPER

SOCIETY

Many belief systems around the world encourage different hairstyles

BOB MARLEY

Long dreadlocks a symbol of the Lion of Judah in Rastafari

High heels were ginally worn by upper ass men to make them look more powerful

Sikhs who do not cut or shave their hair to respect how God made them.

Pink used to be deemed too bright a colour for the delicate constitution of girls ...

HARNAAM KAUR

So how do we know what counts as masculine and feminine at all?

It's no wonder people turn into Worriers, or give it all up and identify as Whatevers ...

TRANSGENDER COMMON MYTHS

By Royal Decree

See also King Monarch on Pages 42-46

* If a transgender creature uses the same bathroom as everyone else, it will open a transdimensional vortex that sucks everyone into the nether realms

* Trans people are secretly giant robots in disguise and can instantly identify each other with a built in transceiver

* There's a magical test and if you don't pass it you don't get your official transgender diploma because you're not trans enough

* Trans people all hate their bodies and have to change everything about themselves until they're unrecognisable

And we're about to meet an extremely powerful lady in Alphabet soup land who proves many of these wrong . . .

Personally, I've got better things to do with my time than to bow to how others think 'a real woman' should be.

Ms President!

SLAM

The Bisexual Bi-lands and Pansexual Pridelands are at war again!

Get me Princess Pan-elope on the line.

Her royal Bi-ness needs to start taking control of the Polysexual Principalities.

So if gender is what goes on inside your head, why does it matter what your body looks like?

Well that's because of these things . . .

GENDER DYSPHORIA . . .

EXTREME UNHAPPINESS WITH PARTS OF YOUR BODY THAT FEEL THE WRONG GENDER TO YOU

Most people have things they want to change about their bodies, but this goes much deeper

SOME EXAMPLES

NOPE

NUH UH

Not liking your chest or other bits

Having too much or too little facial hair

HE SHE IT

People using the wrong pronouns

These affect lots of monsters but are especially important for Transgender and Non binary people.

And as always, it depends on the person.

GENDER EUPHORIA

DELIGHT AT SEEING YOUR BODY AND BEING SEEN BY OTHERS AS THE RIGHT GENDER TO YOU.

SOME EXAMPLES

Being recognised as the right gender by strangers

Yes Ma'am! Why hello, Sir!

Putting on your favourite underwear

Getting the bits you want through surgery, hormones, binding, padding, or other magical means

Being able to stand in the right voice section of a choir

Clive
the
Crossdressing
Centaur

CROSS DRESSING
UNCENTAURED CENTAURS

People who wear clothing typically associated with a different gender

Such sexy hooves

So why do some creatures wear clothes that aren't an expression of the gender they want to be seen as?

Lots of reasons- Wearing clothes you're 'not supposed to' can feel fun, sexy or more comfortable.

What clothes are whose is decided by the society you're in (as we saw on pages 69-70)

Some people cross dress to challenge social norms, parody gender roles or disguise themselves as a different gender

There's centuries of history of cross dressing in theatre, which gave birth to a very visible aspect of gay culture . . .

DRAG LEGENDS

QUEENS, KINGS AND PANTOMIME DAMES

Drag has a long history in entertainment- from Shakespeare plays where the female roles were played by men, to the British pantomime dame.

Drag is about **exaggerated performance** of gender roles, often using makeup, wigs, heels, padding and a **LOT** of glitter to create looks

Many drag artists create stage personas that they embody while in drag. Drag Queens are usually referred to as 'she' and Kings as 'he'.

Outside of drag, people can be male, female, trans, non-binary, gay, lesbian, bisexual, heterosexual, asexual . . . basically anything!

The reasons and style of drag depend on the creature doing it: from fun and fucking with gender, to comedy and creating awareness around important causes

Fred Darling
Keep on Exploring
THIS SATURDAY ONLY
SISTER TWISTER
THE SASS-SQUATCH
LIVE AT THE DRAG DOCKS
HOMOPHOBES AND
HATE-R-OSEXUALS
NEED NOT TURN UP

First Lady Bamfee

the Transfeminine Banshee

ACTIVISM

Activism is an important part of queer history because homosexuality was, and still <u>is</u> illegal in many places

Historically many of the minorities in this book have been lumped together under 'Gay rights'

THE GAY AGENDA
* Changing laws to gain equal rights
* Support and protection from harm
* Increasing social acceptance
* Airing out dirty laundry

But bisexual, trans and particularly transfeminine people have been swept under the rug to make it look more 'normal'

TRANSFEMININE
Someone assigned male at birth whose identity leans towards feminine

For some reason people who break traditional gender roles are very scary to society

Activism is about showing people that there is nothing wrong with being a minority monster, and that creatures of ALL kinds deserve respect, even if you don't understand them.

There are many ways to raise awareness for causes and get stuff DONE

FLAVOURS OF ACTION

* Protest marches
* Pride parades and celebrations
* Giving money or time to charities
* Petitions and letters to government
* Writing, drawing or performing
* Supporting LGBT* movies and books
* Education in schools and workplaces

ALLY COOKIES
A Perfect Recipe

* Several cups of good listening skills
* Entire tin of open mindedness
* A splash of standing up when other people make bad comments
* A pinch of perception for when someone else is more qualified to speak

Serve on the side as allies should not be the main focus of the meal

Even if you're not directly related to a cause you can still help

However it's important to make sure your help is wanted and won't do more harm than good

Welcome to IMPS, old and new faces

Let's go around the room and share times that have been difficult for us this week.

All of the guys that message me on SpellBindr are only into me because they want someone with a big horn to take their purity away

I'm tired of these unicorn stereotypes from movies! Sometimes I feel like I was better off invisible.

My family are fine with my brother having a partner hoard but not me!

Damn double standards!

IT'S NOT ALL RAINBOWS IN ALPHABET SOUP LAND...

Intersectionality is how queer creatures have different experiences depending on

RACE   ETHNICITY   RELIGION

SOCIAL CLASS   NATIONALITY   PHYSICAL ILLNESS

PHYSICAL DISABILITY   MENTAL ILLNESS   AGE

MENTAL DISABILITY

This means that some minority monsters face sexism, racism and many other -isms from within a community that's supposed to support them

And let's not even talk about all the infighting and arguments . . .

Her Royal Bi-ness
Princess Pan-elope
Sigh I knew I should have listened to mum before I got into Poly-tics
the
Polysexual
Pegasus

BI vs PAN

Bisexuals are attracted to their own gender AND to genders not their own

(See pages 9-10)

Pansexuals are attracted to people regardless of their gender

(See pages 23-24)

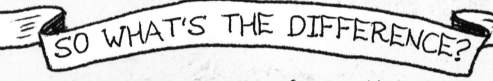

SO WHAT'S THE DIFFERENCE?

They both come under the umbrella of polysexual which covers people who have multiple attractions to different genders

However polysexual often gets mixed up with polyamory which is VERY different
(see pages 13-14)

SO WHAT DO I PICK?

Whichever one suits you most. That's how labels work!

BISEXUAL
More mainstream awareness

Multiple genders
POLYSEXUAL

OMNISEXUAL
All genders

whatever gender
PANSEXUAL

Of course there's an even bigger umbrella term that we've still not covered yet . . .

QUEER

People outside the standard options of sexuality, romance or gender

Queer originally means something strange, odd or different

In the 19th century it became a bad word used to describe creatures from Alphabet Soup Land

However it's since been reclaimed back by some people as a catch all term and identity

It's important that people use it to identify **themselves**, not that it gets chucked **at them**

Queer is gaining popularity as an umbrella term for communities of minority monsters as there's only so long you can make the LGBT acronym

CUPID'S ARROW

CAN STRIKE AT ANY TIME

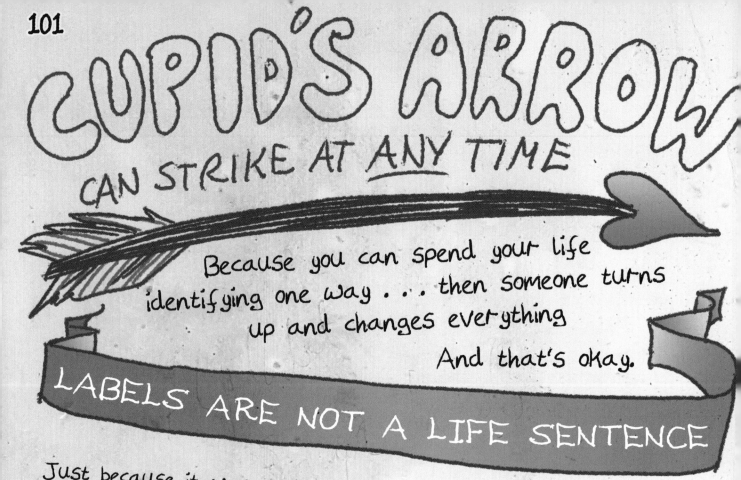

Because you can spend your life identifying one way . . . then someone turns up and changes everything

And that's okay.

LABELS ARE NOT A LIFE SENTENCE

Just because it was a phase doesn't mean it was JUST a phase

Identity is about finding words that describe you right now, and people change all the time.

And there's more to attraction than just the gender of the other person'

Because even if you like someone very much, sometimes you get to the bedroom and it just doesn't work out . . .

THE KINKY CLIFFS

Acts that go beyond 'normal' or vanilla sex to heighten intimacy between the people involved

(And sometimes it's not even about sex)

Here are some examples of common kinks

DRESSING UP

SPANKING

ROLEPLAY

BONDAGE

VOYEURISM

LEATHER

WATERSPORTS

EXHIBITIONISM

WHIPPING

FOOT WORSHIP

RUBBER AND LATEX

SADISM

MASOCHISM

POWER EXCHANGE

DOMINATION

SUBMISSION

Play like this can be risky, which is why consent is extra important

VISIT CONSENT CASTLE!

Impressive, no? Don't worry, it's only a model

How do you know if something is consensual?

Ask yourself- is it a medieval act of war?

* Don't batter down someone's gates- Knock first!
* Don't sneak in during the dead of night- announce your visit
* Don't break your host's rules once inside the Keep
* Leave if you overstay your welcome
* Don't sit outside the drawbridge hoping to slowly wear them down as you cut off their food and supplies.

Good consent is an alliance between nations that benefits everyone

Because if you get it right then it's one hell of a party whenever you visit each other's strongholds

*translation 'pleased to meet you!'

Frank

the Submissive Yeti

DOMINANCE AND SUBMISSION

PEOPLE WHO LIKE TO TAKE CONTROL

PEOPLE WHO LIKE TO GIVE CONTROL TO OTHERS

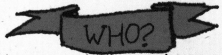

WHO?

Anyone can be a dom or sub. This is an important part of some people's sexuality, some not so much.

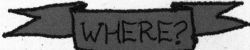

WHERE?

In the bedroom, in a dungeon, on cloud nine- wherever feels sexy (and safe!)

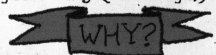

WHY?

Many reasons! Bossing someone about who likes to be bossed about is freeing and fun. Letting someone take over for you can be relaxing.

WHAT?

Whatever the people involved talk about and decide they want to try together.

WHEN?

Varies! Some creatures play only on the odd occasion, some all the time!

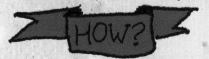

HOW?

Carefully! Kink practitioners encourage the use of communication, safewords and aftercare.

Like all sexuality this is a spectrum. Some people sit at different sides, some both, some neither and some *switch* . . .

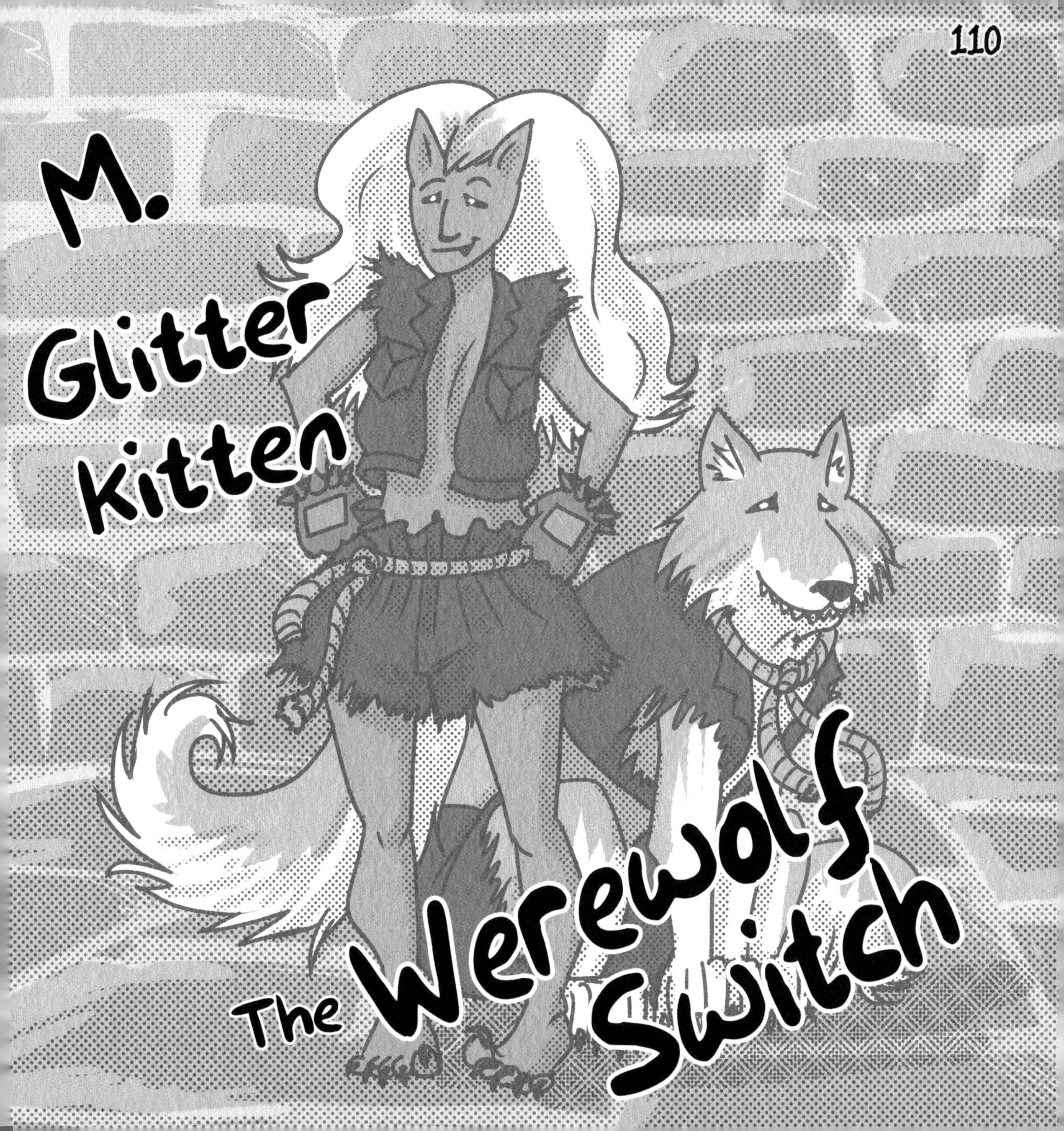

M. Glitter Kitten

The Werewolf Switch

SO WHAT MAKES A MINORITY MONSTER?

Context.

Minority means someone not in the majority . . . and sometimes that's not to do with numbers, but who has all the power.

And there are few more powerful than immortal bloodsucking ~~politicians~~ Vampires

CREEPY-AS-SUCK FOREST

Our journey through Alphabet Soup Land is almost over.

I've learnt so much and realised how much I've yet to learn, but if I had to sum it up I'd say:

THERE'S MORE TO SEXUALITY THAN GENDER

We love, lust and like people for
SO many reasons beyond their gender.
Their voice, their smell, their laugh, their smile.
The way they annoy us, the times they enjoy with us.
Find the people who make you RAWR
and put your claws in them.

AND MORE TO GENDER THAN SEXUALITY

Creatures come in all shapes and sizes
Tall, small, quiet, loud, scaled, feathered and furred.
Male, female, both, between and/or neither
Don't let who you are be dictated
by what you THINK you're supposed to be.
Your adventure is just beginning. Fred Aura
the Explorer

But-but... how can I live in Alphabet Soup Land if I don't have an identity title?

I thought you already had a title?

Huh?

You're Fred Aura the *Explorer*.

Oh.

I suppose I am.

ABOUT THE AUTHOR

Tab Kimpton has been writing queer comics since he was a mini monster.

You can read the rest of his work at DiscordComics.com

Minority monsters started out as a joke about bisexual unicorns being invisible, then became a side project, a series, a Kickstarter and finally the book you hold in your hands.

It just shows that you never know where your adventures will take you.

SPECIAL THANKS

Tab's super squad Karen, Lottie, Alex, Claudia, Harry, Clem, Nathan, and Charlie

Kickstarter video, photography and general BFF Christian

Proof Readers Geoff, Lou, Ted, Shuna and Annette

Punsultants Claire and Bea

And all the brilliant beasts who backed the Kickstarter!

SING ALONG!

Want to play along with the theme tune?
Here are the chords!

C   Am

Welcome to Alphabet Soup land

F   G7

Listen, learn, try to understand

C

These stories of diversity

Am

Behind these myths you will see

F   G7

Minority monsters like you and me

                         C

Like you and me.

Now make up your own verse 🙂

MAKE YOUR OWN MONSTER

COMMON MYTHS

OCEAN OF ROMANTIC NOTIONS
Demisexual Dunes
Consent Castle
The kinky cliffs
Sadomasochism stream
Creepy as FUCK forest
Grey Bay
Prefer-not-Plains
Aromantic Outcropping
Ace cakes
The Flamboyant Forest
Polyamorous Peaks
Desert SEXUAL
ASexuali-Sea
GAYYYYLANDS
Bisexual Beach
Homo Hills
Orgas
TEMP
Polysexual Peninsula
The PolySexual Principalities
Flexible fields
Sappho City
Temple of the QUEER CUPID
Pansexual Pridelands
SEXUALITY SEAS
HERE BE HOMOPHOBES